My First Oxford
Book of Poems

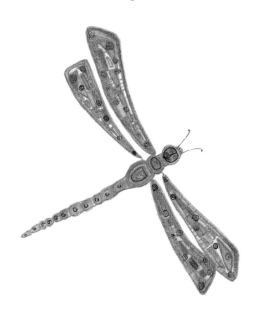

OXFORD
UNIVERSITY PRESS

Great Clarendon Street, Oxford OX2 6DP

Oxford University Press is a department of the
University of Oxford. It furthers the University's
objective of excellence in research, scholarship,
and education by publishing worldwide in

Oxford New York

Athens Auckland Bangkok Bogotá Buenos Aires Calcutta
Cape Town Chennai Dar es Salaam Delhi Florence
Hong Kong Istanbul Karachi Kuala Lumpur Madrid
Melbourne Mexico City Mumbai Nairobi Paris São Paulo
Singapore Taipei Tokyo Toronto Warsaw

with associated companies in Berlin Ibadan

British Library Cataloguing in Publication Data available

ISBN 0-19-276201-X

Printed in Hong Kong

My First Oxford Book of Poems

Compiled by
John Foster

OXFORD
UNIVERSITY PRESS

Contents

Out and About

Creatures

From Dusk till Dawn

Beside the Sea

Fantastical and Nonsensical

Weather and Seasons

Out and About

Out in the Dark and Daylight

Out in the dark and daylight,
under a cloud or tree,

Out in the park and play light,
out where the wind blows free,

Out in the March or May light
with shadows and stars to see,

Out in the dark and daylight . . .
that's where I like to be.

Aileen Fisher

Here is a Field

Here is a field
where dandelions grow,
where silver sails
when breezes blow.

Here is a field
where butterflies feed,
laying their eggs
on the nettles they need.

Here is a field
where rabbits may run
out of their burrows
and into the sun.

Here is a field
where I may lie
in gangling grass
and gaze at the sky.

Celia Warren

The Door

A white door in a hawthorn hedge –
Who lives through there?
A sorcerer? A wicked witch
With serpents in her hair?

A king enchanted into stone?
A lost princess?
A servant girl who works all night
Spinning a cobweb dress?

A queen with slippers made of ice?
I'd love to see.
A white door in a hawthorn hedge –
I wish I had a key.

Richard Edwards

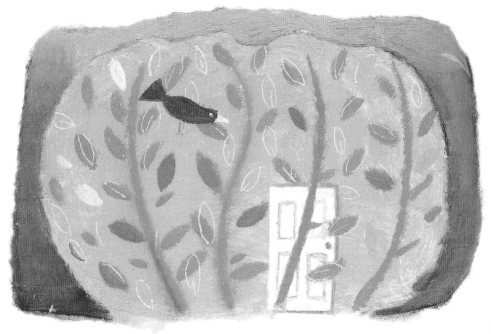

from **A Boy's Song**

Where the pools are bright and deep,
Where the grey trout lies asleep,
Up the river and over the lea,
That's the way for Billy and me.

Where the blackbird sings the latest,
Where the hawthorn blooms the sweetest,
Where the nestlings chirp and flee,
That's the way for Billy and me.

Where the mowers mow the cleanest,
Where the hay lies thick and greenest,
There to trace the homeward bee,
That's the way for Billy and me.

Where the hazel bank is steepest,
Where the shadow falls the deepest,
Where the clustering nuts fall free,
That's the way for Billy and me.

James Hogg

Pond

The pond is green as glass, the water slow,
It barely stirs the frills and fronds of weeds.
Ponds have all day to dream, nowhere to go.

The moorhen bobs and bustles to and fro
To weave a secret nest amongst the reeds.
The pond is green as glass, the water slow.

Bright damselflies like tubes of neon glow
And glitter. Toadspawn trails like strings of beads.
Ponds have all day to dream, nowhere to go.

Pond-skaters dart and water-boatmen row,
Beneath them the great diving beetle feeds.
The pond is green as glass, the water slow.

The smooth newt's egg is laid and left to grow
Wrapped in a leaf each springtime when she breeds.
Ponds have all day to dream, nowhere to go.

With sun to keep it warm, cool mud below,
This place looks after creatures and their needs.
The pond is green as glass, the water slow,
Ponds have all day to dream, nowhere to go.

Sue Cowling

Where Go the Boats?

Dark brown is the river,
  Golden is the sand.
It flows along for ever,
  With trees on either hand.

Green leaves a-floating,
  Castles of the foam,
Boats of mine a-boating –
  Where will all come home?

On goes the river
  And out past the mill,
Away down the valley,
  Away down the hill.

Away down the river,
  A hundred miles or more,
Other little children
  Shall bring my boats ashore.

Robert Louis Stevenson

Clouds

Above me I see mountains,
The mountains of the sky,
They tumble down and spill about
So silently, till I
Can see them change to other things,
For now their shapes evoke
An avalanche of cotton wool
Or puffs of engine smoke.

And now here comes an ogre with
A club clenched in his fist;
His footsteps sound like thunder,
But he fades away in mist.
And now I see a mighty horse,
And now a flock of sheep,
And now I see the shepherd boy
A-lying down to sleep.

Colin West

The Island

They mowed the meadow down below
Our house the other day
But left a grassy island where
We still can go and play.

Right in the middle of the field
It rises green and high;
Bees swing on the clover there,
And butterflies blow by.

It seems a very far-off place
With oceans all around:
The only thing to see is sky,
And wind, the only sound.

Dorothy Aldis

Afternoon

Four o'clock. The afternoon is asleep,
A bee hums in the long grasses,
A hill is white with drowsy sheep;
So slowly each hour passes
With shadows falling on soundless butterfly
Floating into the dreaming sky.

Leonard Clark

14

Hideout

They looked for me
and from my nook
inside the oak
I watched them look.

Through little slits
between the leaves
I saw their looking
legs and sleeves.

They would have looked
all over town
except —
I threw some acorns down.

Aileen Fisher

Dandelions

Over the climbing meadows
Where the swallow shadows float
These are the small gold buttons
On earth's green, windy coat.

Frances Frost

Creatures

The Secret

We have a secret, just we three,
The robin, and I, and the sweet cherry-tree;
The bird told the tree, and the tree told me,
And nobody knows it but just us three.

But of course the robin knows it best,
Because he built the – I shan't tell the rest;
And laid the four little – something in it –
I'm afraid I shall tell it every minute.

But if the tree and the robin don't peep,
I'll try my best the secret to keep;
Though I know when the little birds fly about
Then the whole secret will be out.

Emily Dickinson

Duck's Ditty

All along the backwater,
Through the rushes tall,
Ducks are a-dabbling,
Up tails all!

Ducks' tails, drakes' tails,
Yellow feet a-quiver,
Yellow bills all out of sight
Busy in the river!

Slushy green undergrowth
Where the roach swim –
Here we keep our larder
Cool and full and dim.

Every one for what he likes!
We like to be
Heads down, tails up,
Dabbling free!

High in the blue above
Swifts whirl and call –
We are down a-dabbling,
Up tails all!

Kenneth Grahame

17

The Ladybird

Tiniest of turtles
Your shining back
Is a shell of orange
With spots of black.

How trustingly you walk
Across this land
Of hairgrass and hollows
That is my hand.

Clive Sansom

The Dragonfly

When the heat of the summer
Made drowsy the land,
A dragonfly came
And sat on my hand,
With its blue jointed body,
And wings like spun glass,
It lit on my fingers
As though they were grass.

Eleanor Farjeon

The Caterpillar

Brown and furry
Caterpillar in a hurry;
Take your walk
To the shady leaf or stalk.

May no toad spy you,
May the little birds pass by you;
Spin and die,
To live again a butterfly.

Christina Rossetti

Don't Cry, Caterpillar

Don't cry, Caterpillar
Caterpillar, don't cry
You'll be a butterfly – by and by.

Caterpillar, please
Don't worry 'bout a thing.

'But,' said Caterpillar
'Will I still know myself – in wings?'

Grace Nichols

Snake

Snake slithers
    among stones
       coils and loops
        and hisses
      forked tongue
    darts as fast
as an arrow,
    aims and misses.

Snake glides
    over pebbles,
      sleeps, snoozing
        in the sun,
      hunger long-
    forgotten,
waits still, till
    day is done.

Moira Andrew

Zebra

White men in Africa,
Puffing at their pipes,
Think the zebra's a white horse
With black stripes.

Black men in Africa,
With pipes of different types,
Know the zebra's a black horse
With white stripes.

Gavin Ewart

How Doth the Little Crocodile

How doth the little crocodile
    Improve his shining tail,
And pour the waters of the Nile
    On every golden scale.

How cheerfully he seems to grin,
    How neatly spreads his claws,
And welcomes little fishes in,
    With gently smiling jaws!

Lewis Carroll

Roger the Dog

Asleep he wheezes at his ease.
He only wakes to scratch his fleas.

He hogs the fire, he bakes his head
As if it were a loaf of bread.

He's just a sack of snoring dog.
You can lug him like a log.

You can roll him with your foot,
He'll stay snoring where he's put.

I take him out for exercise,
He rolls in cowclap up to his eyes.

He will not race, he will not romp,
He saves his strength for gobble and chomp.

He'll work as hard as you could wish
Emptying his dinner dish.

Then flops flat, and digs down deep,
Like a miner, into sleep.

Ted Hughes

Cat in the Dark

Look at that!
Look at that!

But when you look
there's no cat.

Without a purr
just a flash of fur
and gone
like a ghost.

The most
you see
are two tiny
green traffic lights
staring at the night.

John Agard

The Snail

At sunset, when the night dews fall,
Out of the ivy on the wall
With horns outstretched and pointed tail
Comes the grey and noiseless snail.
On ivy stems she clambers down,
Carrying her house of brown,
Safe in the dark, no greedy eye
Can her tender body spy,
While she herself, a hungry thief,
Searches out the freshest leaf.
She travels on as best she can
Like a toppling caravan.

James Reeves

Badgers

Badgers come creeping from dark under ground,
   Badgers scratch hard with a bristly sound,
      Badgers go nosing around.

Badgers have whiskers and black and white faces,
   Badger cubs scramble and scrap and run races,
      Badgers like overgrown places.

Badgers don't jump when a vixen screams,
   Badgers drink quietly from moonshiny streams,
      Badgers dig holes in our dreams.

Badgers are working while you and I sleep,
   Pushing their tunnels down twisting and steep,
      Badgers have secrets to keep.

Richard Edwards

Night Spinner

A spider spinning her web one night
Wove in some silver starlight bright
Then caught some drops
Of moon-washed rain
And threaded them
Into a crystal chain.

Crystal and silver
Crystal and silver
Laced between leaves
On the autumn trees.

Silver and crystal
Silver and crystal
Shivering
Shimmering
In the dawn breeze.

Patricia Leighton

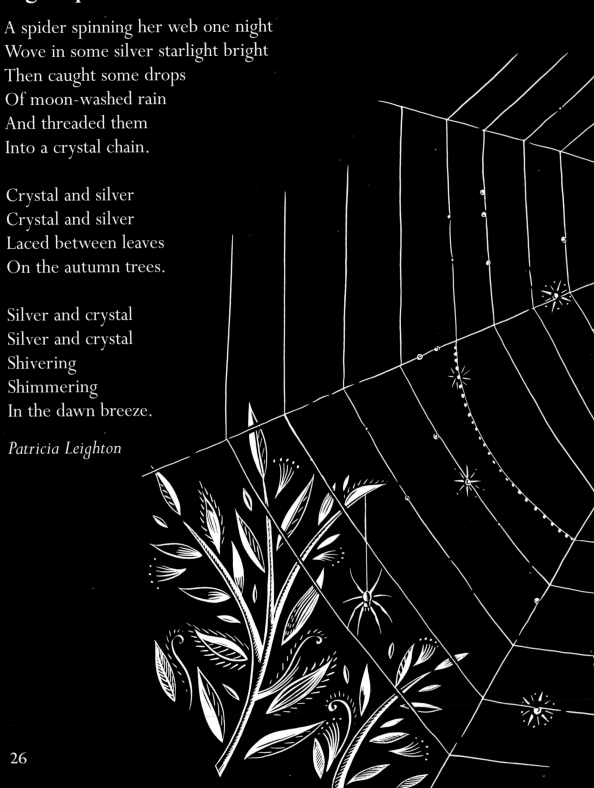

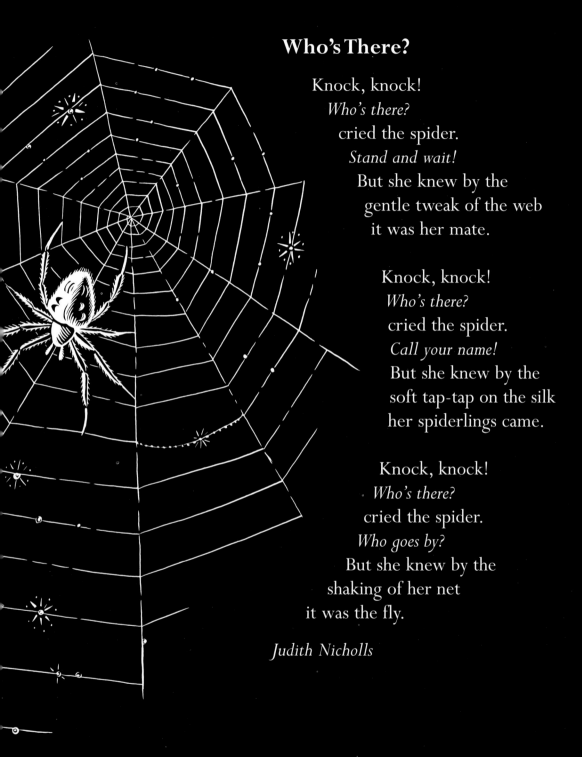

Who's There?

Knock, knock!
Who's there?
cried the spider.
Stand and wait!
But she knew by the
gentle tweak of the web
it was her mate.

Knock, knock!
Who's there?
cried the spider.
Call your name!
But she knew by the
soft tap-tap on the silk
her spiderlings came.

Knock, knock!
Who's there?
cried the spider.
Who goes by?
But she knew by the
shaking of her net
it was the fly.

Judith Nicholls

Old Horses

Old horses,
Leaning on fences.
Old horses,
Rubbing on trees.
Old horses,
Lazy rumps pointing
Towards the cold gusts
Of a southerly breeze.

Old horses,
Never a gallop.
Old horses,
Heavy hoofs slow.
Old horses,
Down by the creek-bed,
Down on the flats
Where the sweet grasses grow.

Old horses,
Sweeping tails twitching.
Old horses,
Tossing their manes.
Old horses,
Gone are the hauling,
The shouts of the driver,
The tug on the reins.

Old horses,
Sleepy heads hanging.
Old horses
Of yesterday's teams.
Old horses,
Soft nostrils breathing
The wheezy contentment
Of hay-scented dreams.

Max Fatchen

The Wild, the Free

With flowing tail, and flying mane,
Wide nostrils never stretched by pain,
Mouths bloodless to the bit or rein,
And feet that iron never shod,
And flanks unscarred by spur or rod,
A thousand horse, the wild, the free,
Like waves that follow o'er the sea.

Lord Byron

Sunning

Old Dog lay in the summer sun
Much too lazy to rise and run.
He flapped an ear
At a buzzing fly;
He winked a half-opened
Sleepy eye;
He scratched himself
On an itching spot;
As he dozed on the porch
When the sun was hot.
He whimpered a bit
From force of habit,
While he lazily dreamed
Of chasing a rabbit.
But Old Dog happily lay in the sun
Much too lazy to rise and run.

James S. Tippett

Peacock

I sit and watch a silver blotch
On yonder lonely hill
The tinkling air grows grey and bare,
The wind blows wet and chill.

The peacock dons his blue and bronze
And under the falling shower
Spreads out his plumes and swiftly blooms
To an enamelled flower.

Harindranath Chattopadhyaya

The Fieldmouse

Where the acorn tumbles down,
   Where the ash tree sheds its berry,
With your fur so soft and brown,
   With your eye so round and merry,
Scarcely moving the long grass,
Fieldmouse, I can see you pass.

Little thing, in what dark den,
   Lie you all the winter sleeping?
Till warm weather comes again,
   Then once more I see you peeping
Round about the tall tree roots,
Nibbling at their fallen fruits.

Fieldmouse, fieldmouse, do not go,
   Where the farmer stacks his treasure,
Find the nut that falls below,
   Eat the acorn at your pleasure,
But you must not steal the grain
He has stacked with so much pain.

Make your hole where mosses spring,
   Underneath the tall oak's shadow,
Pretty, quiet, harmless thing,
   Play about the sunny meadow.
Keep away from corn and house,
None will harm you, little mouse.

Cecil Frances Alexander

The Mouse in the Wainscot

Hush, Suzanne!
Don't lift your cup.
That breath you heard
Is a mouse getting up.

As the mist that steams
From your milk as you sup,
So soft is the sound
Of a mouse getting up.

There! did you hear
His feet pitter-patter,
Lighter than tipping
Of beads in a platter,

And then like a shower
On the window pane
The little feet scampering
Back again?

O falling of feather!
O drift of a leaf!
The mouse in the wainscot
Is dropping asleep.

Ian Serraillier

Allie

Allie, call the birds in,
   The birds from the sky!
Allie calls, Allie sings,
   Down they all fly:
First there came
Two white doves,
   Then a sparrow from his nest,
Then a clucking bantam hen,
   Then a robin red-breast.

Allie, call the beasts in,
   The beasts every one!
Allie calls, Allie sings,
   In they all run:
First there came
Two black lambs
   Then a grunting Berkshire sow,
Then a dog without a tail,
   Then a red and white cow.

34

Dusk till Dawn

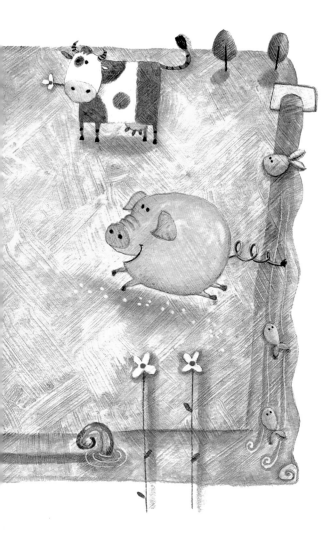

Allie, call the fish up,
　The fish from the stream!
Allie calls, Allie sings,
　Up they all swim:
First there came
Two gold fish,
　A minnow and a miller's thumb,
Then a school of little trout,
　Then the twisting eels come.

Allie, call the children,
　Call them from the green!
Allie calls, Allie sings,
　Soon they run in:
First there came
Tom and Madge,
　Kate and I who'll not forget
How we played by the water's edge
　Till the April sun set.

Robert Graves

Lizzie

Lizzie, Lizzie, spinning top,
Ever dancing, never stop.
Dancing in the morning dew,
Barefoot tap, one two, one two.

Lizzie, Lizzie, spinning top,
Ever dancing, never stop.
Dancing in the sun's warm rays,
Shining brightly at midday.

Lizzie, Lizzie, spinning top,
Ever dancing, never stop.
Dancing as the sun sinks low,
Setting all the lake aglow.

Now she's lying in her bed,
Rosy pillow 'neath her head.
Round the fence a dream comes creeping,
Softly now . . . for Lizzie's sleeping.

Traditional Polish

Song for a Banjo Dance

Shake your brown feet, honey,
Shake your brown feet, chile,
Shake your brown feet, honey,
Shake 'em swift and wil' —
    Get way back, honey,
    Do that rockin' step.
    Slide on over, darling,
        Now! Come out
        With your left.
Shake your brown feet, honey,
Shake 'em, honey chile.

Sun's going down this evening —
Might never rise no mo'.
The sun's going down this very night —
Might never rise no mo'.
So dance with swift feet, honey,
    (The banjo's sobbing low)
Dance with swift feet, honey —
    Might never dance no mo'.

Shake your brown feet, Liza,
Shake 'em, Liza, chile,
Shake your brown feet, Liza,
    (The music's soft and wil')
Shake your brown feet, Liza,
    (The banjo's sobbing low)
The sun's going down this very night —
Might never rise no mo'.

Langston Hughes

Time to go Home

Time to go home!
   Says the great steeple clock.
Time to go home!
   Says the gold weathercock.
Down sinks the sun
   In the valley to sleep;
Lost are the orchards
   In blue shadows deep.
Soft falls the dew
   On cornfield and grass;
Through the dark trees
   The evening airs pass:
Time to go home,
   They murmur and say;
Birds to their homes
   Have all flown away.
Nothing shines now
   But the gold weathercock.
Time to go home!
   Says the great steeple clock.

James Reeves

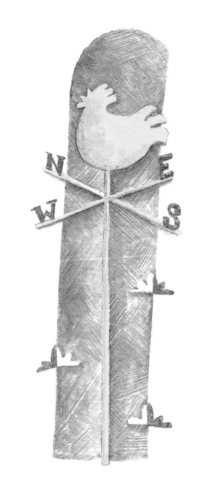

Bedtime

Five minutes, five minutes more, please!
   Let me stay five minutes more!
Can't I just finish the castle
   I'm building here on the floor?
Can't I just finish the story
   I'm reading here in my book?
Can't I just finish the bead-chain –
   It's *almost* finished, look!
Can't I just finish this game, please?
   When a game's once begun
It's a pity never to find out
   Whether you've lost or won.
Can't I just stay five minutes?
   Well, can't I stay just four?
Three minutes, then? two minutes?
   Can't I stay *one* minute more?

Eleanor Farjeon

Something is There

Something is there
   there on the stair
      coming down
         coming down
            stepping with care.
         Coming down
           coming down
              slinkety-sly
Something is coming and wants to get by.

Lilian Moore

Full Moon

Full moon is the nicest time
For telling 'nancy story
Except the ones 'bout snake and ghost
Because they are so scary.

Hide and seek is nice then too
Because it's light as day
And mamas don't say it's too late
If you go out to play.

Odette Thomas

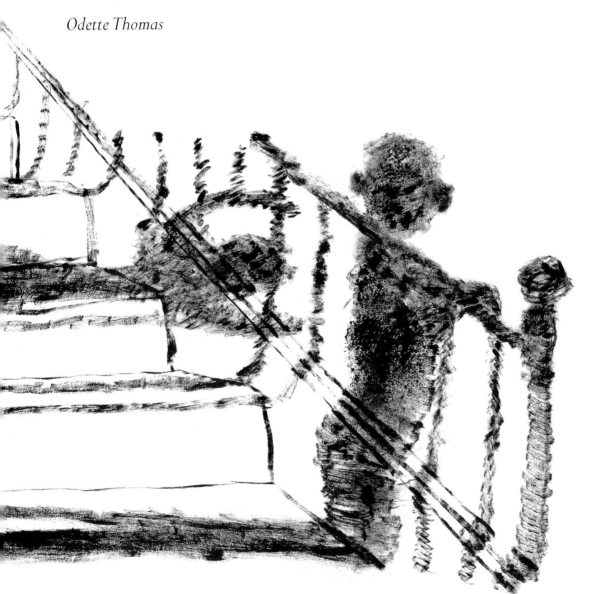

41

In the Dark

I've had my supper,
  And had my supper,
    And HAD my supper and all;
I've heard the story
  Of Cinderella,
    And how she went to the ball;
I've cleaned my teeth,
  And I've said my prayers,
    And I've cleaned and said them right;
And they've all of them been
  And kissed me lots,
    They've all of them said, 'Goodnight.'

So – here I am in the dark alone,
  There's nobody here to see;
    I think to myself,
    I play to myself,
  And nobody knows what I say to myself;
Here I am in the dark alone.
  What is it going to be?
I can think whatever I like to think,
I can play whatever I like to play,
I can laugh whatever I like to laugh,
  There's nobody here but me.

I'm talking to a rabbit . . .
    I'm talking to the sun . . .
I think I am a hundred –
    I'm one.
I'm lying in a forest . . .
    I'm lying in a cave . . .
I'm talking to a Dragon . . .
    I'm BRAVE.
I'm lying on my left side . . .
    I'm lying on my right . . .
I'll play a lot tomorrow . . .

I'll think a lot tomorrow . . .

I'll laugh . . .
    a lot . . .
        tomorrow . . .
        (Heigh-ho!)
            Goodnight.

A. A. Milne

Sweet and Low

Sweet and low, sweet and low,
   Wind of the western sea,
Low, low, breathe and blow,
   Wind of the western sea!
Over the rolling waters go,
Come from the dying moon, and blow,
   Blow him again to me;
While, my little one, while my pretty one sleeps.

Sleep and rest, sleep and rest,
   Father will come to thee soon;
Rest, rest, on mother's breast,
   Father will come to thee soon;
Father will come to his babe in the nest,
Silver sails all out of the west
   Under the silver moon;
Sleep, my little one, sleep my pretty one, sleep.

Alfred, Lord Tennyson

Lullaby

Baby in a basket
floats upon a stream,
rocks along the river
of a gentle dream.

Sails away in slumber
on a cot of rushes
where the lapping of water
soothes and hushes.

Baby in a basket
floats upon a stream,
rocks along the river
of a gentle dream.

Gina Douthwaite

Wynken, Blynken, and Nod

Wynken, Blynken, and Nod one night
   Sailed off in a wooden shoe –
Sailed on a river of crystal light
   Into a sea of dew.
'Where are you going, and what do you wish?'
   The old moon asked the three.
'We have come to fish for the herring fish
   That live in this beautiful sea;
Nets of silver and gold have we!'
     Said Wynken,
     Blynken,
     And Nod.

The old moon laughed and sang a song,
   As they rocked in the wooden shoe;
And the wind that sped them all night long
   Ruffled the waves of dew.
The little stars were the herring fish
   That lived in the beautiful sea –
'Now cast your nets wherever you wish –
   Never afeard are we!'
So cried the stars to the fishermen three,
     Wynken,
     Blynken,
     And Nod.

All night long their nets they threw
    To the stars in the twinkling foam –
Then down from the skies came the wooden shoe,
    Bringing the fishermen home:
'Twas all so pretty a sail, it seemed
    As if it could not be;
And some folk thought 'twas a dream they'd dreamed
    Of sailing that beautiful sea;
But I shall name you the fishermen three:
    Wynken,
    Blynken,
    And Nod.

Wynken and Blynken are two little eyes,
    And Nod is a little head,
And the wooden shoe that sailed the skies
    Is a wee one's trundle-bed;
So shut your eyes while Mother sings
    Of wonderful sights that be,
And you shall see the beautiful things
    As you rock in the misty sea
Where the old shoe rocked the fishermen three:
    Wynken,
    Blynken,
    And Nod.

Eugene Field

Magic Story of Falling Asleep

When the last giant came out of his cave
and his bones turned into the mountain
and his clothes turned into the flowers,

nothing was left but his tooth
which my dad took home in his truck
which my grandad carved into a bed

which my mum tucks me into at night
when I dream of the last giant
when I fall asleep on the mountain.

Nancy Willard

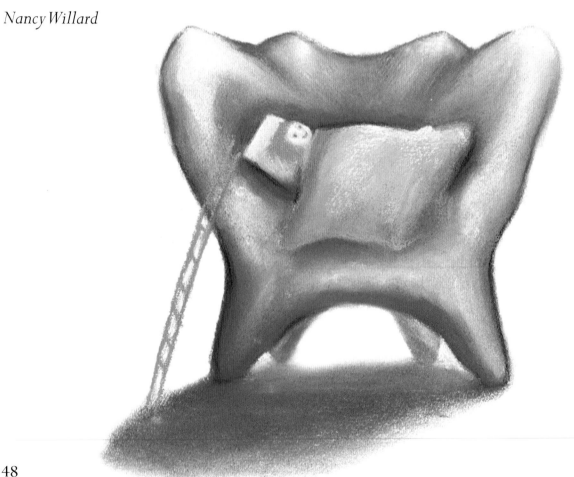

The Falling Star

I saw a star slide down the sky,
Blinding the north as it went by,
Too burning and too hot to hold,
Too lovely to be bought or sold,
Good only to make wishes on
And then forever to be gone.

Sara Teasdale

Windy Nights

Whenever the moon and stars are set,
Whenever the wind is high,
All night long in the dark and wet,
A man goes riding by.
Late in the night when the fires are out,
Why does he gallop and gallop about?

Whenever the trees are crying aloud,
And ships are tossed at sea,
By, on the highway, low and loud,
By at the gallop goes he;
By at the gallop he goes, and then
By he comes back at the gallop again.

Robert Louis Stevenson

The Night Will Never Stay

The night will never stay,
The night will still go by,
Though with a million stars
You pin it to the sky;

Though you bind it with the blowing wind
And buckle it with the moon,
The night will slip away
Like sorrow or a tune.

Eleanor Farjeon

Very Early

When I wake in the early mist
The sun has hardly shown
And everything is still asleep
And I'm awake alone.
The stars are faint and flickering.
The sun is new and shy.
And all the world sleeps quietly
Except the sun and I.
And then the noises start,
The whirrs and huffs and hums,
The birds peep out to find a worm.
The mice squeak out for crumbs,
The calf moos out to find the cow,
And taste the morning air
And everything is wide awake
And running everywhere.
The dew has dried,
The fields are warm,
The day is loud and bright,
And I'm the one who woke the sun
And kissed the stars goodnight.

Karla Kuskin

Early Dawn

The Moon on the one hand,
    the dawn on the other:
The moon is my sister,
    the dawn is my brother.
The moon on my left hand
    the dawn on my right:
My brother, good morning!
    My sister, good night!

Hilaire Belloc

Beside the

Early in the Morning

Early in the morning
The water hits the rocks,
The birds are making noises
Like old alarum clocks.
The soldier on the skyline
Fires a golden gun
And over the back of the chimney-stack
Explodes the silent sun.

Charles Causley

Sea

Seashell

Shell at my ear –
come share how I hear
busy old sea in whispers.

Moans rise from ancient depths
in ocean sighs
like bands of ghost monsters.

Waves lash and fall –
in roars and a squall
with all a mystery ahhh!

James Berry

Sounds of the Sea

Sometimes the sea sighs
When it breathes easy.
Sometimes when angry
It rises up
With a deafening roar
And smashes against
The sandy floor.
Sometimes the evening breeze
Makes it smoothly flow
To sleepily slap
On the silvery shore.

Ann Marie Linden

The Sea

Deep glass-green seas
chew rocks
with their green-glass jaws.
But little waves
creep in
and nibble softly at the sand.

Lilith Norman

Long, Lone

Long, long, long and lone
is the selkie's song when the storm winds moan,
is the sigh of the sea as it rubs the stone,
is the word of the sea that lives in the bone.

Long and lone is the gliding flight
of the albatross in the dawn's grey light
on its wide white wings where the winds blow high
over the waves where the sea-ghosts cry.

Long and lone is the sea I find
that sighs on the shore at the edge of my mind;
long, long, long and lone
is the word of the sea that lives in the bone.

Russell Hoban

The Caribbean Calling

Listen to the kiskadee singing!
The bamboo bawling!
The humming-bird humming,
Sweet and low.
Listen to the sea splashing!
The black-birds calling,
The sound of pick-axe and hoe!
Listen to the children playing,
Sunlight brightening their faces,
Smiling at mangoes and cocoa.
Listen to the Caribbean calling
Its children wherever they roam
Back to their landscape home.

Faustin Charles

Mine

I made a sand castle.
In rolled the sea.
    'All sand castles
    belong to me —
        to me,'
said the sea.

I dug sand tunnels.
In flowed the sea.
    'All sand tunnels
    belong to me —
        to me,'
said the sea.

I saw my sand pail floating free.
I ran and snatched it from the sea.
    'My sand pail
    belongs to me —
        to ME!'

Lilian Moore

Song of the Seashore

The soft waves lisp,
On the stone-spangled shore,
Shining and shimmering,
Murmuring 'More . . .
More music, please . . .'
And the stones sigh and ride
And whisper their songs
To the incoming tide.

Daphne Lister

Little Fish

The tiny fish enjoy themselves
in the sea.
Quick little splinters of life,
their little lives are fun to them
in the sea.

D. H. Lawrence

Grim and Gloomy

Oh, grim and gloomy
So grim and gloomy
Are the caves beneath the sea.
Oh, rare but roomy
And bare and boomy,
Those salt sea caverns be.

Oh, slim and slimy
Or grey and grimy
Are the animals of the sea.
Salt and oozy
And safe and snoozy
The caves where those animals be.

Hark to the shuffling,
Huge and snuffling,
Ravenous, cavernous,
Great sea-beasts!
But fair and fabulous,
Tintinnabulous,
Gay and fabulous are their feasts.

Ah, but the queen of the sea,
The querulous, perilous sea!
How the curls of her tresses
The pearls on her dresses,
Sway and swirl in the waves,
How cosy and dozy,
How sweet ring-a-rosy
Her bower in the deep sea-caves.

Oh, rare but roomy
And bare and boomy
Those caverns under the sea,
And grave and grandiose,
Safe and sandiose
The dens of her denizens be.

James Reeves

The Tide Rises, The Tide Falls

The tide rises, the tide falls,
The twilight darkens, the curlew calls;
Along the sea-sands damp and brown
The traveller hastens towards the town,
   And the tide rises, the tide falls.

Darkness settles on roofs and walls,
But the sea, the sea in the darkness calls;
The little waves, with their soft white hands,
Efface the footprints in the sands,
   And the tide rises, the tide falls.

The morning breaks; the steeds in their stalls
Stamp and neigh, as the hostler calls;
The day returns, but nevermore
Returns the traveller to the shore,
   And the tide rises, the tide falls.

Henry Wadsworth Longfellow

Roadways

One road leads to London,
    One road runs to Wales,
My road leads me seawards
    To the white dipping sails.

One road leads to the river,
    As it goes singing slow;
My road leads to shipping,
    Where the bronzed sailors go.

Leads me, lures me, calls me
    To salt, green, tossing sea;
A road without earth's road-dust
    Is the right road for me.

A wet road, heaving, shining,
    And wild with seagulls' cries,
A mad salt sea-wind blowing
    The salt spray in my eyes.

My road calls me, lures me
    West, east, south, and north;
Most roads lead men homewards,
    My road leads me forth.

To add more miles to the tally
    Of grey miles left behind,
In quest of that one beauty
    God put me here to find.

John Masefield

63

If I Could Have a Pair of Wings

If I could have a pair of wings,
  Do you suppose that I
Would choose a pair of robin's wings
  And skim across the sky;
Or would I take the wings of gulls
  And glide across the seas;
Or would I buzz around the flowers
  With wings of busy bees?
I could, with wings of dragonflies,
  Dart over lakes and creeks;
Or with a pair of eagle's wings
  Soar over mountain peaks.
Perhaps, with wings of butterflies,
  I'd flutter out of sight;
But with mosquito wings, I guess,
  I'd flit about and bite.

Anita E. Posey

Fantastical

Tartary

If I were Lord of Tartary,
    Myself and me alone,
My bed should be of ivory,
    Of beaten gold my throne;
And in my court should peacocks flaunt,
And in my forests tigers haunt,
And in my pools great fishes slant
    Their fins athwart the sun.

If I were Lord of Tartary,
    Trumpeters every day
To every meal should summon me,
    And in my courtyard bray;
And in the evening lamps would shine,
Yellow as honey, red as wine,
While harp, and flute, and mandoline
    Made music sweet and gay . . .

Walter de la Mare

*and
Nonsensical*

Cow

The Cow comes home swinging
Her udder and singing:

'The dirt O the dirt
It does me no hurt.

And a good splash of muck
Is a blessing of luck.

O I splosh through the mud
But the breath of my cud

Is sweeter than silk.
O I splush through manure

But my heart stays pure
As a pitcher of milk.'

Ted Hughes

The Owl and the Pussy-Cat

The Owl and the Pussy-Cat went to sea
  In a beautiful pea-green boat,
They took some honey, and plenty of money,
  Wrapped up in a five-pound note.
The Owl looked up to the stars above,
  And sang to a small guitar,
'O lovely Pussy! O Pussy, my love,
  What a beautiful Pussy you are,
    You are,
    You are!
  What a beautiful Pussy you are!'

Pussy said to the Owl, 'You elegant fowl!
  How charmingly sweet you sing!
O let us be married! too long we have tarried:
  But what shall we do for a ring?'
They sailed away for a year and a day,
  To the land where the Bong-tree grows,
And there in a wood a Piggy-wig stood,
  With a ring at the end of his nose,
    His nose,
    His nose,
  With a ring at the end of his nose.

'Dear Pig, are you willing to sell for one shilling
   Your ring?' Said the Piggy, 'I will.'
So they took it away, and were married next day
   By the Turkey who lives on the hill.
They dined on mince, and slices of quince,
   Which they ate with a runcible spoon;
And hand in hand, on the edge of the sand,
   They danced by the light of the moon,
      The moon,
      The moon,
   They danced by the light of the moon.

Edward Lear

Silly Old Baboon

There was a Baboon
Who, one afternoon,
Said, 'I think I will fly to the sun.'
So, with two great palms
Strapped to his arms,
He started his take-off run.

Mile after mile
He galloped in style
But never once left the ground.
'You're running too slow,'
Said a passing crow,
'Try reaching the speed of sound.'

So he put on a spurt –
By God how it hurt!
The soles of his feet caught fire.
There were great clouds of steam
As he raced through a stream
But he still didn't get any higher.

Racing on through the night,
Both his knees caught alight
And smoke billowed out from his rear.
Quick to his aid
Came a fire brigade
Who chased him for over a year.

Many moons passed by.
Did Baboon ever fly?
Did he ever get to the sun?
I've just heard today
That he's well on his way!
He'll be passing through Acton at one.

Spike Milligan

PS. Well, what do you expect from a Baboon?

The Flattered Flying-Fish

Said the Shark to the Flying-Fish over
    the phone:
'Will you join me tonight? I am
    dining alone.
Let me order a nice little dinner
    for two!
And come as you are, in your
    shimmering blue.'

Said the Flying-Fish: 'Fancy
    remembering me,
And the dress that I wore at the
    Porpoises' tea!'
'How could I forget?' said the Shark
    in his guile:
'I expect you at eight!' and rang off
    with a smile.

She has powdered her nose,
    she has put on her things;
She is off with one flap of her
    luminous wings.
O little one, lovely, light-hearted
    and vain,
The Moon will not shine on your beauty
    again!

E.V. Rieu

Mesopotamia

I dreamed I was sailing on dusty waters
   Mesopotamia Mesopotamia
There were two yellow rivers merged into one river
   Mesopotamia Mesopotamia
My boat had a woven cabin for shade
And a double golden sail like an eagle in flight
And a woman who sang to me like marmalade
As we sailed in the direction of the night.

Adrian Mitchell

Adventures of Isabel

Isabel met an enormous bear,
Isabel, Isabel, didn't care;
The bear was hungry, the bear was ravenous,
The bear's big mouth was cruel and cavernous.
The bear said, Isabel, glad to meet you,
How do, Isabel, now I'll eat you!
Isabel, Isabel, didn't worry,
Isabel didn't scream or scurry.
She washed her hands and she straightened her hair up,
Then Isabel quietly ate the bear up.

Once in a night as black as pitch
Isabel met a wicked old witch.
The witch's face was cross and wrinkled,
The witch's gums with teeth were sprinkled.
Ho ho, Isabel! the old witch crowed,
I'll turn you into an ugly toad!
Isabel, Isabel, didn't worry,
Isabel didn't scream or scurry.
She showed no rage and she showed no rancor,
But she turned the witch into milk and drank her.

Isabel met a hideous giant,
Isabel continued self reliant.
The giant was hairy, the giant was horrid,
He had one eye in the middle of his forehead.
Good morning, Isabel, the giant said,
I'll grind your bones to make my bread.
Isabel, Isabel, didn't worry,
Isabel didn't scream or scurry.
She nibbled the zwieback that she always fed off,
And when it was gone, she cut the giant's head off.

Isabel met a troublesome doctor,
He punched and he poked till he really shocked her.
The doctor's talk was of coughs and chills
And the doctor's satchel bulged with pills.
The doctor said unto Isabel,
Swallow this, it will make you well.
Isabel, Isabel, didn't worry,
Isabel didn't scream or scurry.
She took those pills from the pill concocter,
And Isabel calmly cured the doctor.

Ogden Nash

Unicorn

The Unicorn with the long white horn
    Is beautiful and wild.
He gallops across the forest green
So quickly that he's seldom seen
Where Peacocks their blue feathers preen
    And strawberries grow wild.
He flees the hunter and the hounds,
Upon black earth his white hoof pounds,
Over cold mountain streams he bounds
    And comes to a meadow mild.
There, when he kneels to take his nap,
He lays his head in a lady's lap
    As gently as a child.

William Jay Smith

The Dragon Hunt

'Let's hunt for dragons,' Rachel said,
'Tonight, before we go to bed.'
So each of us, quiet as a mouse,
Hunted and searched around the house.
We looked under tables,
We looked under chairs,
We looked behind curtains
And under the stairs,
We looked in the corners
Of all of the rooms,
We peeped in the cupboard
Behind all the brooms,
We looked in the wardrobe
And under the bed,
'No, not a dragon in sight,' Rachel said.

But even so, when I curled up that night,
I felt a bit twitchy and tingly with fright,
For though we had looked simply *every*where,
I was sure a dragon was hiding *some*where!

Daphne Lister

Weather Seasons

Weather

January new beginning,
Resolutions,
Snowflakes spinning.

February frosty fogs,
Winter shivers,
Fire-warm logs.

March blows windy, smells of spring,
Leaves peek out,
Brave blackbirds sing.

April showers fall soft and slow,
Earth wakes up,
And green things grow.

May Day ribbons round a pole,
May-time babies,
Lamb and foal.

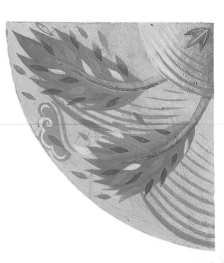

and

June brings summer blazing in,
    Scent of roses,
    Sun on skin.

July joy means school is out,
    Time for picnics,
    Heat and drought.

August goes on holiday,
    Sandy castles,
    Friends to stay.

September sees the autumn come,
    Plough the fields
    One by one.

October gales lash the trees,
    Leaves a-swirling,
    Crashing seas.

November nights all crisp and cold,
    Winter coats
    For young and old.

December dark, yet full of light,
    Christmas carols,
    Star so bright.

Lucy Coats

Winter

When icicles hang by the wall,
   And Dick the shepherd blows his nail,
And Tom bears logs into the hall,
   And milk comes frozen home in pail;
When blood is nipped, and ways be foul
Then nightly sings the staring owl
    Tu-whit, tu-who – a merry note;
While greasy Joan doth keel the pot.

When all aloud the wind doth blow,
   And coughing drowns the parson's saw,
And birds sit brooding in the snow,
   And Marian's nose looks red and raw,
When roasted crabs hiss in the bowl,
Then nightly sings the staring owl
   Tu-whit, tu-who – a merry note,
While greasy Joan doth keel the pot.

William Shakespeare

January

The days are short,
   The sun a spark
Hung thin between
   The dark and dark.

Fat snowy footsteps
   Track the floor,
And parkas pile up
   Near the door.

The river is
   A frozen place
Held still beneath
   The trees' black lace.

The sky is low.
   The wind is gray.
The radiator
   Purrs all day.

John Updike

White Fields

I
In the winter time we go
Walking in the fields of snow;

Where there is no grass at all;
Where the top of every wall,

Every fence, and every tree,
Is as white as white can be.

II
Pointing out the way we came,
– Every one of them the same –

All across the fields there be
Prints in silver filigree;

And our mothers always know,
By the footprints in the snow,

Where it is the children go.

James Stephens

Robin

If on a frosty morning
the robin redbreast calls
his waistcoat red and burning
like a beggar at your walls

throw breadcrumbs on the grass for him
when the ground is hard and still
for in his breast there is a flame
that winter cannot kill.

Iain Crichton Smith

A Change in the Year

It is the first mild day of March:
    Each minute sweeter than before,
The redbreast sings from the tall larch
    That stands beside our door.

There is a blessing in the air,
    Which seems a sense of joy to yield
To the bare trees, and mountains bare;
    And grass in the green field.

William Wordsworth

Bluebells

This year and every year
The long-legged trees
Stand, now spring is here,
In a bright blue sea.

No one can count the bluebells
That gather together
Until they fill
The woods with waves of their colour.

Beneath new shining leaves
On the long-legged trees
Children gathering flowers
Paddle in a bluebell sea.

Stanley Cook

Rainbows

A rainbow is a painted smile
   turned upside down.
It's a multi-coloured bridge
   spanning the streets of town.

A rainbow is a brilliant band
   across my sister's hair.
It's a fluorescent mountain
   piercing the morning air.

A rainbow is a skipping rope
   for our playground game.
It's a splash of coloured ink
   lighting the sky with flame.

A rainbow is a promise
   made before time grew old.
It's a mysterious magic place
   hiding a pot of gold.

Moira Andrew

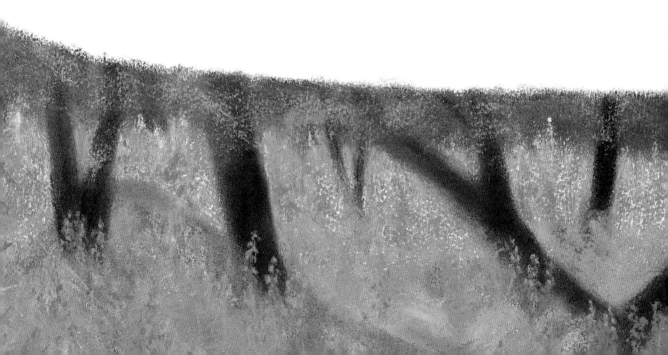

August Afternoon

Where shall we go?
    What shall we play?
What shall we do
    On a hot summer day?

We'll sit in the swing.
    Go low. Go high.
And drink lemonade
    Till the glass is dry.

One straw for you,
    One straw for me,
In the cool green shade
    Of the walnut tree.

Marion Edey

Fly Away, Swallow

Fly away, fly away, over the sea,
Sun-loving swallow, for summer is done.
Come again, come again, come back to me,
Bringing the summer and bringing the sun.

Christina Rossetti

The Winter Warrior

I heard the winter warrior riding by,
I heard his chariot in the night's chill sky,
Its ice-wheels rattled while the wind did blow,
Scattering hail – ice-gravel – on the earth below.

I felt the coldness as he rode roughly past,
His snowy ice-shod horses, racing fast,
Went by my window, then, gone in a trice,
Only the patterns of their breath left, etched in ice.

Daphne Lister

December Leaves

The fallen leaves are cornflakes
That fill the lawn's wide dish.
And night and noon
The wind's a spoon
That stirs them with a swish,

The sky's a silver sifter
A-sifting white and slow,
That gently shakes
On crisp brown flakes
The sugar known as snow.

Kaye Starbird

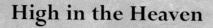

High in the Heaven

High in the Heaven
A gold star burns
Lighting our way
As the great world turns.

Silver the frost
It shines on the stem
As we now journey
To Bethlehem.

White is the ice
At our feet as we tread,
Pointing a path
To the manger-bed.

Charles Causley

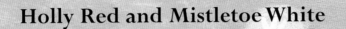

Holly Red and Mistletoe White

Holly red and mistletoe white,
The stars are shining with golden light,
Burning like candles this Holy Night,
Holly red and mistletoe white.

Mistletoe white and holly red,
The doors are shut and the children a-bed,
Fairies at foot and angels at head,
Mistletoe white and holly red.

Alison Uttley

The Waiting Game

Nuts and marbles in the toe,
An orange in the heel,
A Christmas stocking in the dark
Is wonderful to feel.

Shadowy, bulging length of leg
That crackles when you clutch,
A Christmas stocking in the dark
Is marvellous to touch.

You lie back on your pillow
But that shape's still hanging there.
A Christmas stocking in the dark
Is very hard to bear,

So try to get to sleep again
And chase the hours away.
A Christmas stocking in the dark
Must wait for Christmas Day.

John Mole

A Footprint on the Air

'Stay!' said the child. The bird said, 'No
My wing has mended, I must go.
I shall come back to see you though,
One night, one day – '
    'How shall I know?'
'Look for my footprint in the snow.'

'The snow soon goes – oh, that's not fair!'
'Don't grieve. Don't grieve. I shall be there
In the bright season of the year,
One night, one day – '
    'But tell me, where?'
'Look for my footprint on the air.'

Naomi Lewis

The World with its Countries

The world with its countries,
Mountains and seas,
People and creatures,
Flowers and trees,
The fish in the waters,
The birds in the air
Are calling to ask us
All to take care.

These are our treasures,
A gift from above,
We should say thank you
With a care that shows love
For the blue of the ocean,
The clearness of air,
The wonder of forests
And the valleys so fair.

The song of the skylark,
The warmth of the sun,
The rushing of clear streams
And new life begun
Are gifts we should cherish,
So join in the call
To strive to preserve them
For the future of all.

John Cotton

Index of Authors

Index of Titles and First Lines

Acknowledgements

We are grateful to the authors for permission to include the following poems, all of which are published for the first time in this collection.

Moira Andrew: 'Snake', copyright © Moira Andrew 2000; **James Berry**: 'Seashell', copyright © James Berry 2000; **Faustin Charles**: 'The Caribbean Calling', copyright © Faustin Charles 2000; **Sue Cowling**: 'Pond', copyright © Sue Cowling 2000; **Gina Douthwaite**: 'Lullaby', copyright © Gina Douthwaite 2000; **Richard Edwards**: 'The Door' and 'Badgers', both copyright © Richard Edwards 2000; **Patricia Leighton**: 'Night Spinner', copyright © Patricia Leighton 2000; **Daphne Lister**: 'The Dragon Hunt' and 'The Winter Warrior', both copyright © Daphne Lister 2000; **Iain Crichton Smith**: 'Robin', copyright © 2000; **Celia Warren**: 'Here is a Field', copyright © Celia Warren 2000; **Nancy Willard**: 'Magic Story of Falling Asleep,' copyright © Nancy Willard 2000, by permission of Jean V. Naggar Literary Agency on behalf of the author.

We also acknowledge permission to include previously published poems: **Dorothy Aldis**: 'The Island' from *Hop, Skip and Jump!*, © 1934, renewed © 1961 Dorothy Aldis, reprinted by permission of G.P. Putnam's Sons, a division of Penguin Putnam Inc; **Moira Andrew**: 'Rainbows', first published in *Rainbow Year* (Belair Publications Ltd, 1994), © Moira Andrew 1994, reprinted by permission of the author; **John Agard**: 'Cat in the Dark' from *I Din Do Nuttin* (Bodley Head Children's Books), reprinted by permission of the publisher; **Hilaire Belloc**: 'Early Dawn' from *Complete Verse* (Random House Group), reprinted by permission of The Peters Fraser and Dunlop Group Limited on behalf of The Estate of Hilaire Belloc; **Charles Causley**: 'Early in the Morning' and 'High in the Heaven' from *Collected Poems* (Macmillan Books), reprinted by permission of David Higham Associates; **Leonard Clark**: 'Afternoon' reprinted by permission of the Literary Executor of Leonard Clark; **Lucy Coats**: 'Weather' first published in *First Rhymes* (Orchard Books, a division of the Watts Publishing Group), reprinted by permission of the publisher; **Stanley Cook**: 'Bluebells' first published in *The Squirrel in Town* (Blackie, 1988), copyright © The Estate of Stanley Cook, reprinted by permission of Sarah Matthews; **John Cotton**: 'The World with its Countries' first published in *Wake Up, Stir About* (Unwin Hyman, 1989), reprinted by permission of the author; **Walter de la Mare**: 'Tartary' from *The Complete Poems of Walter de la Mare* (UK, 1969/USA 1970) reprinted by permission The Literary Trustees of Walter de la Mare, and the Society of Authors as their representative; **Marion Edey**: 'August Afternoon' from *Open the Door* by Marion Edey and Dorothy Grider (Charles Scribner's Sons, New York, 1949), reprinted by permission of Atheneum Books for Young Readers, an imprint of Simon & Schuster Children's Publishing Division; **Gavin Ewart**: 'Zebra' from *Learned Hippopotamus* (Hutchinson), reprinted by permission of Margo Ewart; **Eleanor Farjeon**: 'Bedtime', 'The Night Will Never Stay', and 'The Dragonfly' from *Something I Remember* (Puffin Books), reprinted by permission of David Higham Associates; **Max Fatchen**: 'Old Horses' from *A Pocketful of Rhymes* (Puffin Books), reprinted by permission of John Johnson Agents; **Aileen Fisher**: 'Hideout' from *In the Woods, In the Meadow, In the Sky* (Charles Scribner's Sons, 1965), © 1965 Aileen Fisher, © renewed 1993; and 'Out in the Dark and Daylight' from *Out in the Dark and Daylight*, both reprinted by permission of Marian Reiner, Literary Agent; **Kenneth Grahame**: 'Duck's Ditty' from *The Wind in the Willows* (Methuen Books), copyright The University Chest, Oxford, reprinted by permission of Curtis Brown, London; **Robert Graves**: 'Allie' from *Complete Poems* (Carcanet Press Ltd, 1975), reprinted by permission of the publisher; **Russell Hoban**: 'Long, Lone' from *The Last of the Wallendas* (Hodder & Stoughton), reprinted by permission of David Higham Associates; **Langston Hughes**: 'Song for a Banjo Dance' from *The Collected Poems of Langston Hughes* (Vintage Publishers, USA), © 1994 by The Estate of Langston Hughes, reprinted by permission of David Higham Associates and Alfred A. Knopf Inc; **Ted Hughes**: 'Roger the Dog' from *What is the Truth* and 'Cow' from *Collected Animal Poems: Volume 1, The Iron Wolf* (1995), reprinted by permission of the publishers Faber & Faber Ltd. **Karla Kuskin**: 'Very Early' from *In the Middle of the Trees*, © 1959, renewed 1986 by Karla Kuskin, reprinted by permission of S©ott Treimel New York; **D.H. Lawrence**: 'Little Fishes' from *The Complete Poems of D.H. Lawrence* edited by V. de Sola Pinto and F.W. Roberts, copyright © 1964, 1971 Angelo Ravagli and C.M. Weekley, Executors of the Estate of Frieda Lawrence Ravagli, reprinted by permission of Laurence Pollinger Limited and the Estate of Frieda Lawrence Ravagli and Viking Penguin, a division of Penguin Putnam Inc; **Naomi Lewis**: 'A Footprint on the Air' from *He Said, She Said* edited by Anne Harvey (Blackie), reprinted by permission of the author; **Daphne Lister**: 'Songs of the Seashore' from *Gingerbread Pigs and Other Rhymes* (Transworld Publications Ltd 1980), copyright © Daphne Lister 1980, reprinted by permission of the author; **John Masefield**: 'Roadways' from *Collected Poems* (Heinemann), reprinted by permission of The Society of Authors as the literary representatives of the Estate of John Masefield; **Spike Milligan**: 'Silly Old Baboon' from *A Book of Milliganimals* (Puffin Books), reprinted by permission of Spike Milligan Productions Ltd; **A.A. Milne**: 'In the Dark' from *Now We Are Six* (Methuen), copyright 1927 by E.P. Dutton, renewed © 1955 by A.A. Milne, copyright under the Berne Convention, reprinted by permission of Dutton Children's Books, a division of Penguin Putnam Inc. and Egmont Children's Books Limited, London; **Lilian Moore**: 'Mine' from *I Feel the Same Way* (Atheneum, 1967), © 1967, 1995 by Lilian Moore, reprinted by permission of Marian Reiner Literary Agent, for the author; 'Something in There' from *Spooky Rhymes and Riddles* (1972), © 1972 by Lilian Moore, reprinted by permission of Scholastic, Inc.; **Adrian Mitchell**: 'Mesopotamia' from *Balloon Lagoon and the Magic Islands of Poetry* (Orchard Books, 1997), copyright © Adrian Mitchell 1997, reprinted by permission of The Peters Fraser and Dunlop Group Limited on behalf of Adrian Mitchell. Educational Health Warning! Adrian Mitchell asks that none of his poems are used in connection with any examination whatsoever; **John Mole**: 'The Waiting Game' from *Catching the Spider* (Blackie), reprinted by permission of the author; **Ogden Nash**: 'Adventures of Isabel' from *Candy is Dandy: the Best of Ogden Nash* (first published in 1936 by Little Brown, and in Great Britain in 1988 by Andre Deutsch Ltd), copyright © 1936 by Ogden Nash, renewed, reprinted by permission of Curtis Brown, Ltd, New York, and the publishers; **Grace Nichols**: 'Don't Cry, Caterpillar' from *No Hickory, No Dickory, No Dock*, (Viking, 1991), © Grace Nichols 1991, reprinted by permission of Curtis Brown Ltd, London, on behalf of Grace Nichols; **Judith Nicholls**: 'Who's There' from *Midnight Forest* (Faber & Faber, 1987), © Judith Nicholls 1987, reprinted by permission of the author; **James Reeves**: 'Time to Go Home', 'Grim and Gloomy', and 'The Snail' from *Complete Poems for Children* (Heinemann), © James Reeves, reprinted by permission of Laura Cecil Literary Agency on behalf of the James Reeves Estate; **E.V. Rieu**: 'The Flattered Flying-Fish' from *The Flattered Flying Fish* (Methuen Children's Books, an imprint of Egmont Children's Books Limited, 1962), © The Estate of E.V. Rieu 1962, reprinted by permission of David Higham Associates; **Clive Sansom**: 'Ladybird' from *Collected Poems* (Methuen Books), reprinted by permission of David Higham Associates; **Ian Serraillier**: 'The Mouse in the Wainscot' from *The Monster Horse* (Oxford University Press), reprinted by permission of Anne Serraillier; **William Jay Smith**: 'Unicorn' from *Laughing Time: Collected Nonsense* (Farrar, Straus & Giroux, Inc, 1990), copyright © 1990 by William Jay Smith, reprinted by permission of the publisher; **James Stephens**: 'White Fields' from *Collected Poems* (Macmillan), reprinted by permission of The Society of Authors as the literary representatives of the Estate of James Stephens; **Sara Teasdale**: 'The Falling Star' from *The Collected Poems of Sara Teasdale*, copyright 1930 by Sara Teasdale Filsinger, copyright © renewed 1958 by Guaranty Trust Co. of New York, Executor, reprinted by permission of Simon & Schuster; **Odette Thomas**: 'Full Moon' from *Rain Falling, Sun Shining*, reprinted by permission of Bogle L'Ouverture Press; **John Updike**: 'January' from *A Child's Calendar*, copyright © 1965, 1999 by John Updike, all rights reserved, reprinted by permission of Holiday House, Inc. **Alison Uttley**: 'Holly Red and Mistletoe White' from *Little Grey Rabbit's Christmas*, reprinted by permission of HarperCollins Publishers Ltd; **Colin West**: 'Clouds' from *A Moment in Rhyme* (Hutchinson, 1987), copyright © Colin West 1987, reprinted by permission of the author. Although we have tried to trace and contact copyright holders before publication, in some cases this has not been possible. If contacted we will be pleased to rectify any errors or omissions at the earliest opportunity.

The illustrations are by:
Lucy Alcock pp.1, 14–15, 18–19, 20–21, 30–31, 76–77, 90–91, 93. **Lindsey Gardiner** pp.16–17, 74–75. **Mary McQuillan** pp.2–3, 4–5, 34–35, 38–39, 46–47, 60–61, 66–67, 94, 96, 70–71. **Julie Monks** pp.8–9, 42–43, 53, 62–63, 65, 81, 82–83, 88–89, 95. **Liz Pyle** pp.6–7, 44–45, 48–49, 50–51, 84–85, 92. **Gary Taylor** pp.28–29, 36, 40–41, 72–73, 86–87. **Suzanne Watts** pp.12–13, 22–23, 33, 54–55, 58–59, 68–69. **Sarah Young** pp.10–11, 24–25, 26–27, 57, 78–79. **Cover Illustration** by Graham Percy